# YOUR KNOWLEDGE HAS VALUE

- We will publish your bachelor's and master's thesis, essays and papers

- Your own eBook and book - sold worldwide in all relevant shops

- Earn money with each sale

Upload your text at www.GRIN.com and publish for free

**Bibliographic information published by the German National Library:**

The German National Library lists this publication in the National Bibliography; detailed bibliographic data are available on the Internet at http://dnb.dnb.de .

This book is copyright material and must not be copied, reproduced, transferred, distributed, leased, licensed or publicly performed or used in any way except as specifically permitted in writing by the publishers, as allowed under the terms and conditions under which it was purchased or as strictly permitted by applicable copyright law. Any unauthorized distribution or use of this text may be a direct infringement of the author s and publisher s rights and those responsible may be liable in law accordingly.

**Imprint:**

Copyright © 2018 GRIN Verlag
Print and binding: Books on Demand GmbH, Norderstedt Germany
ISBN: 9783668689466

**This book at GRIN:**

https://www.grin.com/document/421545

Weronika Krawczyk

# The effectiveness of aid in promoting economic development in developing countries

GRIN Verlag

**GRIN - Your knowledge has value**

Since its foundation in 1998, GRIN has specialized in publishing academic texts by students, college teachers and other academics as e-book and printed book. The website www.grin.com is an ideal platform for presenting term papers, final papers, scientific essays, dissertations and specialist books.

**Visit us on the internet:**

http://www.grin.com/

http://www.facebook.com/grincom

http://www.twitter.com/grin_com

# The effectiveness of aid in promoting economic development in developing countries.

by Weronika Krawczyk

University of Reading

United Kingdom

01.2018

Poverty is a very complex and multidimensional phenomenon. The World Bank (2016) defines it generally as the lack of multiple assets and resources necessary for material well-being leading to physical deprivation and social exclusion. According to its statistics 1 in 10 people in the world live for less than $1,90 a day. And, while the situation in Asia improved in absolute terms mainly due to massive progress in China and India, Sub-Saharan Africa still lags behind. In fact, according to Sir Paul Collier (2008) the world's poorest African countries are nowadays worse off than they had been in 1970s. Reducing poverty is as complex as the poverty itself. In most cases it requires radical institutional changes leading towards freedom to participate in society, enforcement of property rights, provision of public goods as well as of social infrastructure. Ultimately, it is about giving incentives and opportunities to the poorest part of society so that it can participate in the economy (Acemoglu, 2003). In numerous cases where governments were unsuccessful at combating the poverty, international aid has partly filled this vacuum.

Yet, the aid per se has failed to be a remedy for persistent poverty and will never be the latter. According to Acemoglu and Robinson (2014) the belief that large capital inflows in the form of foreign aid can eradicate poverty for good has been a predominant theory of economic development as well as leading ideology of governments and aid agencies over the past six decades. The economists criticise this approach as being short-sighted and overlooking the importance of inclusive domestic institutions needed to generate growth and to lift the societies out of poverty. What is more, numerous scholars argue that foreign aid is and has always been allocated purposively and strategically to serve geopolitical interests of the donors (Collier, 2008; Milner and Tingley, 2010, 2013; Apodaca, 2017). This selection bias has additionally exacerbated the already weak impact of foreign aid on the economic development and poverty eradication. Last but not least, aid fungibility, i.e. the problem of using aid for purposes different than intended as well as tying it as mechanism to deal with it also impact its effectiveness.

Scholars such as Rodrik (2013) and Collier (2008) emphasise the importance of institutions being a fundamental causal factor for a developing country to rise out of poverty. Collier (2008) argues that while the aid might be particularly effective in short-term growth stimulation for post-conflict situations, it will not be effective in generating growth in the long term unless obstacles to it such as poor governance and policy will be dealt with. This thesis is supported by Rodrik (2013) who conditions long-term growth upon accumulation of fundamental capabilities such as human capital and institutions. The latter that focus on securing large elites will be growth oriented while the ones securing narrow elites will choose wealth redistribution (Collier, 2017). What is more, well designed policies will attract private capital that usually is not provided by aid. This capital is crucial for rising up productivity of a developing country (Collier, 2008). This process referred to as structural transformation resulting in rapid industrialisation has almost always been the stimulus of the extraordinarily high economic growth in developing countries (Rodrik, 2013).

Extractive institutions that act in their narrow interests are the problem in many poor and developing countries. These institutions will be likely to use the aid for similarly narrow purposes. There is substantial evidence that a lot of foreign aid has been misused by recipient governments. Those in power tend to loot public money and get it abroad. Nigeria, the 6th largest producer of petroleum, is an example of a country that despite having massive natural and human resources at its disposal has failed to secure the basic economic infrastructure to its citizens. The oil revenues as well as aid have been misused over the past decades by subsequent dictatorship governments for private purposes at the expense of the public. Consequently, Nigeria now possesses a stark dichotomy of wealth and poverty (Frieden et al, 2016). The country that has asked the international community for $ 1.2 billion aid last year, has been plagued by corruption (Boseley, 2016). It is estimated that Nigerians held abroad around $ 100 billion of capital by the end of military rules in 1998 (Collier, 2008). Paradoxically, as a consequence of such practices, poor countries that lack capital, have integrated into global economy through capital flight instead of capital inflows (Collier, 2008).

While the official rhetoric of governments focuses on poverty reduction, human welfare improvement and development as main purposes of giving aid, the academic research has determined that foreign aid has been given predominantly to promote geostrategic interests. Historically, aid was a tool of Western states to contain the spread of communism and to deter growth of the Soviet Union (Apodaca, 2017). The tendency to allocate aid according to the characteristics and interests of the donors rather than of the recipients is a fact. And, consequently foreign aid is and has always been an important element of foreign policy for many countries (Milner and Tingley, 2013). This leads to a situation where aid less tends to be channeled to countries that need it the most. It is instead given to countries where donors have strong political and trade relations, investment interests or colonial ties. Additionally, the agency problem is what also determines the selection bias. As a consequence of this aid tends to bypass the neediest countries with the highest risks (Collier, 2008).

The USA has been the largest aid donor in absolute numbers. In 2011 it spent $31 billion on foreign assistance (Milner and Tingley, 2013). American leaders and policy makers have always viewed foreign assistance as an essential instrument of foreign policy that has been increasingly associated with national security (Tarnoff and Lawson, 2016 cited in Apodaca, 2017). An example of Haiti clearly shows that the aid given to it officially to boost economic development and improve the situation of its citizens has proved elusive. After having received approximately $38 billion in aid since mid-1950s Haiti remains underdeveloped and poor (Buss, 2015). First, the American leaders driven by vested interests have used the aid to support 30 years of brutal regime of the Duvaliers because they provided the USA a counterbalance to the communist Cuban dictatorship in the region. Then, the aid was channeled to a country characterised by weak institutions and corruption (Buss, 2015). Consequently, subsequent Haitian leaders would loot and misuse the aid what translated into instability of and insecurity in its provision as an American stance.

The Haitian example demonstrates that foreign assistance can be a very flexible tool of pursuing the policy that serves mostly the donor interests. It can be provided as a reward for specific behaviour or as an inducement to change it. It can also be suspended as a means of punishing or coercing the recipient. As argued by Tarnoff and Lawson (2016) in Apodaca (2017) it can be an instrument for influencing events, solving certain issues and projecting the US (or any other donor's) values. Decisions on its allocation are made by political leaders of the donor country and as shown by Milner and Tingley (2010) in their research foreign aid policy is not only driven by geopolitical agenda but also by domestic interests of the donor. They argue that presidents have to construct aid policy in such a way as to get the majority support for it in the United States Congress and that the legislators consider the effects of aid on their districts and vote accordingly. This is also where interests of different groups come into play in the form of lobbying. Hence, foreign aid is and has been highly politicised.

While bilateral aid is criticised for being used predominantly to promote the donor's objectives and geostrategic interests, it is multilateral aid that is believed to be less politically biased. Advocates of the use of aid as foreign policy tool prefer bilateral aid because it allows the donor to have complete control over it, and because its receipt leaves the recipient obligated to the donor. At the same time, multilateral aid is believed to be cheaper, to disperse accountability as well as to be more politically neutral and needs-driven (Apodaca, 2017). Over time aid has evolved from bilateral donor-recipient based relationships to multilateral ventures involving international organizations such as the World Bank (WB), the International Monetary Fund (IMF), the Organisation for Economic Co-operation and Development (OECD) or the United Nations Development Programme (UNDP). Since the 1990s the multilateral aid has averaged approximately 30 per cent of the total economic aid and yet the USA has historically delivered much less than the above average- 12 per cent- of its aid multilaterally (Milner and Tingley, 2013).

The research conducted by Biscaye et al (2015) for the Bill & Melinda Gates Foundation shows that generally the bilateral aid given directly to recipient governments is used in vast majority of cases for debt relief. This according to the authors indicates that it may be more politically viable for the donors to provide the bilateral aid for the purposes of debt forgiveness versus new cash funding. Furthermore, according to the research bilateral ODA given to the public sector is used predominantly to finance environment, infrastructure as well as water and sanitation projects. And, while the relative allocation to most subsectors of social infrastructure and services is similar for both bilateral and multilateral aid, a much larger percentage of multilateral aid is dedicated to health. These findings appear to support the commonly accepted hypothesis that bilateral aid is less likely to be development-oriented than multilateral aid (Burnside and Dollar, 2000; Ram, 2003; Minoiu and Reddy, 2007; Rajan and Subramanian, 2010 cited in Biscaye et al 2015).

What is more, multilateral aid is believed to be more effective at realising desired development outcomes because multilateral agencies are able to exercise pro-poor conditionality more effectively than bilateral agencies can (Rodrik, 1995 cited in Biscaye et al 2015). And, since multilateral agencies have been historically committed to promoting development outcomes they have a greater incentive to impose pro-development conditions for the recipient countries, such as the preparation of the Poverty Reduction Strategy Papers (PRSPs). On the other hand, however, some evidence exists that multilateral agencies are not impartial either when granting aid. A research of Kaja and Werker (2010) cited in Apodaca (2017) found that members of the executive board of the International Bank for Reconstruction and Development (IBRD) received approximately two times more funding than its non-members. What is more, another research has shown that the IBRD loans were influenced by a recipient government's temporary seat in the UN Security Council (Dreher et al, 2009; Kuziemko and Werker, 2006 cited in Apodaca, 2017).

Therefore, as argued above, by providing aid assistance donors, both foreign governments and international organizations, try to in a certain manner influence recipients' domestic institutions and their public expenditure policies. On the other hand, however, both critics and advocates of foreign aid have been concerned that recipients can easily alter the donors' intentions in regard to their expenditure patterns (Pack and Pack, 1993). If a government undertakes a donor-financed project in the circumstances of the absence of such financing from domestic budget, then donor's aid relaxes the government's budget constraints. On the other hand, though, if a recipient government had budgeted certain expenditure, the aid received to finance the latter releases the government's resources that can be spent on potentially unsustainable project or on undesirable purpose. Collier and Hoeffler (2007) cited in Apodaca (2017) have found out that approximately additional 40 per cent on the top of general military spending in Africa is financed by the aid received from the OECD because of aid fungibility.

This is why scholars and donors have been concerned about the aid fungibility problem and about the ways to avoid it. The analysis conducted by Pack and Pack (1993) did not find an evidence of fungibility across sectoral expenditures in the case of Indonesia. However, the same scholars found substantial diversion of foreign aid away from its intended purposes in the case of Dominican Republic. Contrary to the donors' objectives, the shift of funds from development expenditures to deficit reduction, debt service and tax relief was identified. The radical difference between these two studies' outcomes was according to authors due to the importance of public aid contribution to gross domestic product. While foreign aid accounted for on average 4 per cent of Indonesian GDP, it made up approximately 1 per cent of GDP of the Dominican Republic. Hence, the more important the aid is as a source of public revenues, the greater the ability of the donors to monitor its use (Pack and Pack, 1993).

While looking at the aid contribution to GDP might be one of the ways of identifying the recipient's improper behaviour, it is tying aid to conditions for its use that has arisen as a strategy of dealing with aid fungibility problem (Milner and Tingley, 2013). Yet, ex ante policy conditionality of the aid as an incentive for policy improvement has been criticised as the one having a disastrous opposite effect (Collier, 2008). Not only it promotes the recipient's disobeyance of the rules and provisions but it also impacts accountability. In the case of Nigeria the policy conditionality resulted in building a mass of misinformed citizens (Collier, 2017). The Nigerian government domestically blamed Washington for the cuts implemented even if it kept receiving money from it. At the same time it modified its policies superficially to show an apparent reform effort, and it still got the desired redistributive effect of the looted aid. While ex ante policy conditionality has in fact proved to support dysfunctional policies leading to misusing the aid, the ex post governance conditionality aimed to award good governance is believed to be more successful in terms of impact (Collier, 2008).

Yet, aside from the purpose of influencing the recipient's conduct the aid can be tied because of commercial motives in an attempt to increase business opportunities of the donor. It is estimated that historically the USA has tied approximately 75 per cent, Greece 70 per cent while Canada and Austria 40 per cent of their aid (Radelet, 2006 cited in Apodaca, 2017). On the other hand, Norway, Ireland and the United Kingdom do not practise tying their aid at all. It is reported that, overall, approximately 50 per cent of ODA is being tied in a manner, and that this process reduces its value by up to 30 per cent (Riddell, 2014 cited in Apodaca, 2017). While tying aid to certain expenditures by the donors allows them to ensure that funds are spent on specific projects, at the same time it may reduce the value of the aid because it prevents the recipient from purchasing the best value for money. Furthermore, in this context the aid is a means of exerting influence including very often a political one on the recipient because otherwise it may be cut.

There is no consensus in the scholastic literature on whether bilateral or multilateral aid is more effective at supporting positive development and social outcomes (Biscaye et al 2015). However, there is empirical evidence that these two aid flows differ substantially in terms of development orientation, control over aid, accountability to donors, ability to impose conditionality, potential for aid to foster private investment, perceived legitimacy of aid flows among recipients as well as cost-effectiveness. In relative terms though, multilateral aid is the one that is more politically neutral, motivated by altruistic motives, needs-oriented, and thus more focused on getting the development outcomes. Given the fact, it is on the rise as a proportion of total aid in the recent years, it is important this tendency is sustained unless aid can be allocated bilaterally on the basis of needs. Moreover, the problem of aid fungibility should be dealt with and tying aid as the most commonly used mechanism to mitigate it should be used only to the extent required for the latter.

What is more, scientists are in agreement on the fact that it is poor performance in terms of governance, economy management and public resources spending that impedes economic growth and keeps the society impoverished. Empirical evidence on aid effectiveness shows that good governance is influenced by reasons that have little to do with foreign aid flows (Lancaster, 2006). There is numerous historical evidence of aid supporting dysfunctional regimes and extractive institutions because this has been politically profitable for the donors. Therefore, it is important that aid is politically neutral and conditioned upon the good governance in its ex post form, i.e. that aid supports the visible and viable effort of a country trying to reform its institutions in order to escape bad governance and poverty traps. Moreover, donors have tendency to favour some countries over others. Such an attitude may put the underprivileged countries at a disadvantage. Therefore, aid should be given based on needs not on connections.

In order to make a difference, aid should be a means, not an end it itself. It should be a means of promoting inclusive institutions and sound policies focused on fostering development and creating civil society. Besides, it should be a means of attracting private capital and of incentivising pioneer investments because this is what developing countries need the most. Aid should also help support connecting the developing states into global economy by financing very expensive projects such as building physical infrastructure and supporting urbanization. In order to work, it should be distributed consistently and long-term because economic development that aid is aimed at supporting is a slow process. Humanitarian assistance can make an ad hoc difference in the lives of people in the developing world. Yet, sustained economic development provides the best alternative of lifting poor countries out of poverty. This is what all donors should bear in mind.

**Bibliography:**

Acemoglu, D., 2003. *Root Causes: A historical approach to assessing the role of institutions in economic development* [online]. Finance & Development. Available from: http://www.imf.org/external/pubs/ft/fandd/2003/06/pdf/acemoglu.pdf [Accessed 02.01.2018].

Acemoglu D. and Robinson J.A., 2014. *Why foreign aid fails – and how to really help Africa* [online]. The Spectator, 25 Jan. 2014. Available from: https://www.spectator.co.uk/2014/01/why-aid-fails/ [Accessed 02.01.2018].

Apodaca, C., 2017. *Foreign Aid as Foreign Policy Tool* [online]. Oxford Research Encyclopedia of Politics. Available from: http://politics.oxfordre.com/view/10.1093/acrefore/9780190228637.001.0001/acrefore-9780190228637-e-332#.WlEMoBUF8vY [Accessed 05.01.2018].

Biscaye P., Panhorst Harris K., Reynolds T. and Anderson C.L., 2015. *Relative Effectiveness of Bilateral and Multilateral Aid on Development and Social Outcomes* [online]. Evans School of Public Affairs, University of Washington, Seattle. Available from: https://evans.uw.edu/sites/default/files/public/EPAR_UW_294_Multilateral%20vs%20Bilateral%20Aid_3.30.15.pdf [Accessed 05.01.2018].

Boseley S., 2016. *Money from Nigeria laundered in UK 'should go to help starving children'* [online]. The Guardian, 2 Dec. 2016. Available from: https://www.theguardian.com/world/2016/dec/02/money-from-nigeria-laundered-in-uk-should-go-to-helping-starving-children [Accessed: 02.01.2018]

Buss, T.F., 2015. *Foreign Aid and the Failure of State Building in Haiti from 1957 to 2015* [online]. Latin American Policy Journal, Vol. 6, Issue 2, pp. 319–339. Available from: http://onlinelibrary.wiley.com/doi/10.1111/lamp.12080/abstract [Accessed 06.01.2018].

Collier, P., 2008. *The Bottom Billion: Why the Poorest Countries Are Failing and What Can Be Done About It.* Oxford: Oxford University Press.

Collier, P., 2017. *From Poverty to Prosperity: Understanding Economic Development* MOOC [online]. University of Oxford, Oxford. Available from: https://www.edx.org/course/poverty-prosperity-understanding-oxfordx-oxbsg01x-0 [Accessed: 02.01.2018]

Frieden, J., Lake D. and Schultz K., 2016. *World Politics: Interests, Interactions, Institutions.* International Student Edition, New York and London: W.W. Norton & Company Inc.

IBRD, 2016. *Poverty and Shared Prosperity 2016: Talking on Inequality* [online]. World Bank Group. Available from: http://www.worldbank.org/en/publication/poverty-and-shared-prosperity [Accessed 06.01.2018].

Lancaster C., 2006. *Failing and Failed States: Toward a Framework for U.S. Assistance* In *Short of the Goal: U.S. Policy and Poorly Performing States* [online]. Center for Global Development, Washington, pp. 285-305. Available from: https://www.cgdev.org/sites/default/files/9781933286051-Birdsall-Vaishnav-Ayres-short-of-goal.pdf [Accessed 03.01.2018].

Milner H.V. and Tingley D., 2010. *The Political Economy of U.S. Foreign Aid: American Legislators and the Domestics Politics of Aid* [online]. Harvard University, Cambridge. Available from: https://scholar.harvard.edu/files/dtingley/files/enp.pdf [Accessed 03.01.2018].

Milner H.V. and Tigley D., 2013. *Introduction to Geopolitics of Foreign Aid* [online]. Harvard University, Cambridge. Available from: https://scholar.harvard.edu/dtingley/publications/introduction-geopolitics-foreign-aid [Accessed 03.01.2018].

Pack H. and Pack Rothenberg J., 1993. *Foreign Aid and the Question of Fungibility* [online]. The Review of Economics and Statistics Vol. 75, No. 2, pp. 258-265. Available from: https://www.jstor.org/stable/2109431 [Accessed 03.01.2018].

Rodrik D., 2013. *The Past, Present, and Future of Economic Growth* [online]. Global Citizen Foundation Working Paper; John F. Kennedy School of Government, Harvard University, Cambridge. Available from: https://drodrik.scholar.harvard.edu/publications/past-present-and-future-economic-growth [Accessed 02.01.2018].

# YOUR KNOWLEDGE HAS VALUE

- We will publish your bachelor's and master's thesis, essays and papers

- Your own eBook and book -
  sold worldwide in all relevant shops

- Earn money with each sale

Upload your text at www.GRIN.com
and publish for free